MAKING METRIC
MEASUREMENTS

Neil Ardley

Series consultant: Professor Eric Laithwaite

Franklin Watts

London New York Toronto Sydney

The author
Neil Ardley gained a degree in science and worked as
a research chemist and patent agent before entering
publishing. He is now a full-time writer and is the
author of more than fifty information books on
science, natural history and music.

The consultant
Eric Laithwaite is Professor of Heavy Electrical
Engineering at Imperial College, London. A well-
known television personality and broadcaster, he is
best known for his inventions on linear motors.

© 1983 Franklin Watts Ltd

First published in Great
Britain in 1983 by
Franklin Watts Ltd
12a Golden Square
London W1

First published in the United
States of America by
Franklin Watts Inc.
387 Park Avenue South
New York
N.Y. 10016

Printed in Belgium

UK edition:
ISBN 0 86313 025 9
US edition:
ISBN 0-531-04615-X
Library of Congress
Catalog Card Number:
82-62991

Designed by
David Jefferis

Illustrated by Janos Marffy,
Hayward Art Group and
Arthur Tims

ACTION SCIENCE

MAKING METRIC MEASUREMENTS

Contents

Equipment

Apart from pencil and paper and a few everyday items, you will need the following equipment to carry out the activities in this book.

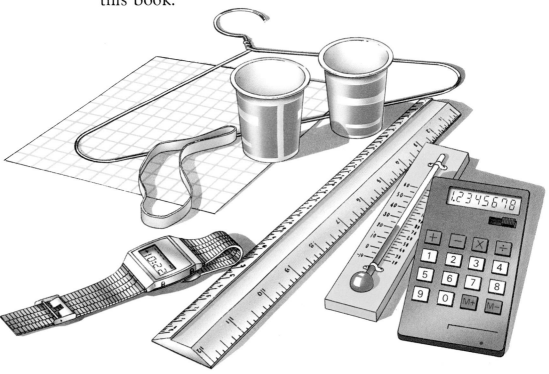

Calculator
Cartons
Coat-hanger
Graph paper
Kitchen scales
Marbles
Measuring jug
Paper clip

Poster paint
Rubber band
Ruler
Tape measure
Thermometer
Watch showing seconds
Weights (in grams and
    kilograms)

Introduction

To find out how and why things work, we often need to measure what happens first. And knowing how to use metric measurements is becoming more and more important. Most forms of science depend on metric measurement. To make many things we need to measure lengths metrically. To cook with metrics, we need to weigh ingredients and measure both time and temperature.

The activities in this book include projects for constructing simple measuring instruments, and for making measurements and understanding how to use metric units.

Most of the projects include an example that gives the actual measurements and result obtained when the experiment was performed. The example shows you how to get the result. You may need to use a calculator to work out an answer from the measurements. The calculator will give you an answer to many decimal places. Remember that the methods used here are not accurate to this degree. Use only the first two or three numbers shown.

✴ This symbol appears throughout the book. It shows you where to find a scientific explanation of each activity.

Measuring weight

mark

There are two ways of finding out how heavy things are.

Use sticky tape to fix the cartons.

Coat-hanger balance

Attach two empty yoghurt cartons to the ends of a wire coat-hanger. Hang it over a nail in a post so that it can swing freely. Let the hanger come to rest, and then make a mark on the post below the end of the hook. Place an object in one carton, and put weights into the other carton until the hanger balances and the hook comes back to the mark.

☀ The balance rests at the mark when the contents of each carton have the same weight. The weight of the object is therefore equal to the total of the weights in the other carton.

△ With this method of weighing, you compare the weight of an object with standard weights. These are weights in grams and kilograms. However, you could use marbles instead of weights and find how many marbles equal the weight of an object.

6

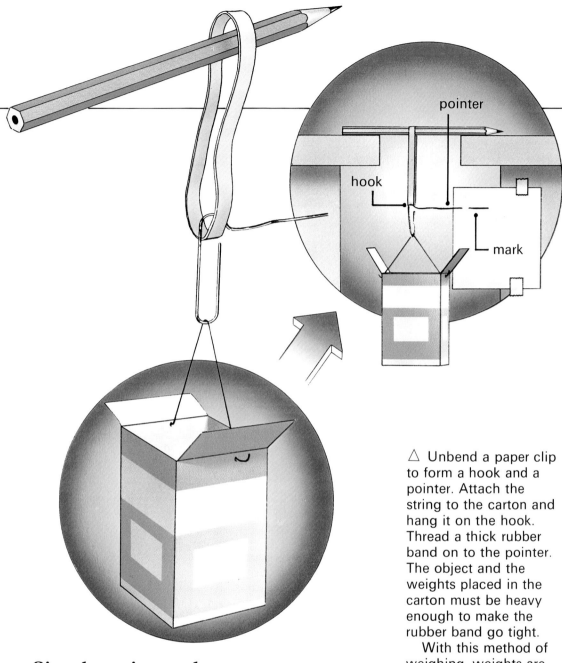

pointer

hook

mark

Simple spring scales

Make some scales with a rubber band, paper clip, string and milk carton as shown. Hang the scales from a pencil placed across two desks and put a weight inside. Tape some paper to the side of one

△ Unbend a paper clip to form a hook and a pointer. Attach the string to the carton and hang it on the hook. Thread a thick rubber band on to the pointer. The object and the weights placed in the carton must be heavy enough to make the rubber band go tight.

With this method of weighing, weights are needed only to make the scales and check that they are correct. By making the object move a pointer along a scale, objects of any weight on the scale can be weighed.

▽ The paper with the marks given by the two weights in the example.

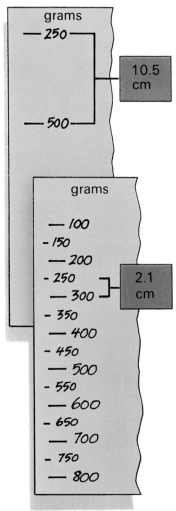

△ The paper with the scale drawn from the marks.

desk so that the paper clip pointer rests near the top of the paper. Mark this position and repeat with a heavier weight. Remove the paper and draw a scale on it as described in the example. Then put the paper back in the same position. Place an object in the carton. The pointer will indicate its weight on the scale.

❉ The weight of the object makes the rubber band stretch by a certain amount depending on how heavy it is. The weights show how much the band stretches. By drawing a scale, the amount of stretch can be used to measure the weight of any object.

Example

Weights used: 250 g and 500 g.
Distance between marks given by each weight = 10.5 cm. This distance measures the difference between the two weights, which is 500 − 250 = 250 g. To mark scale in intervals of 50 g, find number of intervals between marks. This is 250 ÷ 50 = 5. Size of each interval is 10.5 ÷ 5 = 2.1 cm. Scale marked in divisions 2.1 cm apart from 100 g to 800 g.
These scales are accurate to about 20 g. This means that the true weight could be up to 10 g more or less than the weight indicated on the scales.

Measuring time

Make a pendulum to measure time and adjust it until it is accurate.

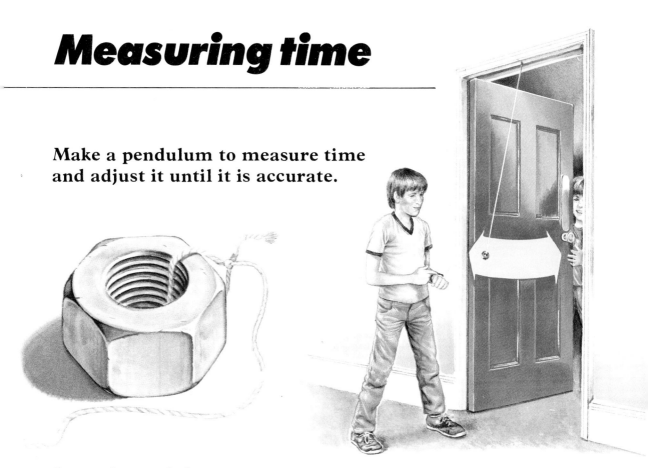

Seconds pendulum

Tie a heavy metal nut or similar object to the end of a long piece of string. Fasten the string to a high shelf or door frame so that the nut is 1 meter below. Swing this pendulum and time it with a watch that shows seconds. Adjust the length of the string until each swing, either to or fro, takes exactly 1 second.

✳ A pendulum always swings to and fro in the same time however large or small the swing. The time of each swing depends only on the length of the pendulum.

△ Use a drawing pin to fasten the string. Time 20 swings and adjust the pendulum until they take 20 seconds. Lengthen the string to make each swing last longer, or shorten it to speed up the pendulum. In this way, the pendulum can be adjusted until it is as accurate as the watch. Many measuring instruments are checked by testing them with an accurate measurement.

Decimals and units

Find out how to use decimal measurements and units.

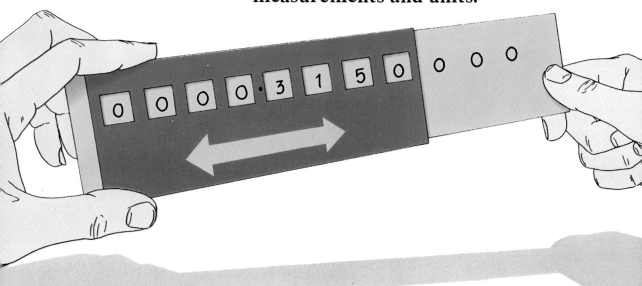

Decimal number slide

Make the decimal number slide shown by following the instructions in the caption. Insert a long strip of paper and write a measurement such as 315, which is the weight of this book in grams. Write the figures in three of the holes so that the decimal point is in the right place. Then write zero in all the other holes. To change the measurement to other decimal units, slide the strip in or out. Move it one number to the left to multiply by 10, and one number to the right to divide by 10.

△ Fold a piece of paper into three and cut eight square holes in the middle. Take care when using scissors. Put a large dot between the fourth and fifth holes to show the decimal point.

Here the slide has been moved to show 0.315, which is the weight of this book in kilograms.

10

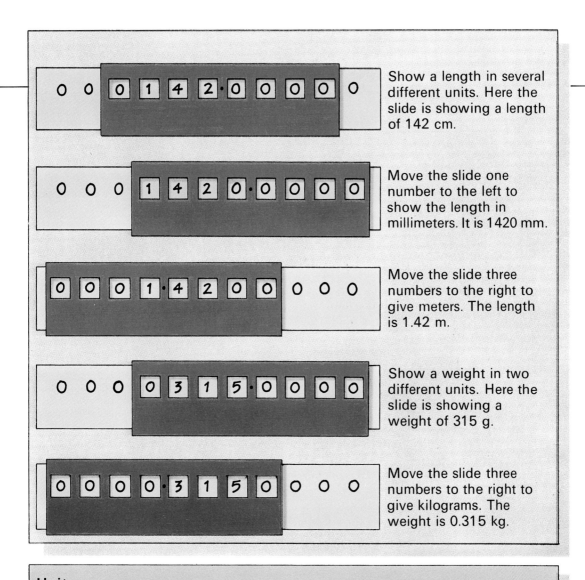

Show a length in several different units. Here the slide is showing a length of 142 cm.

Move the slide one number to the left to show the length in millimeters. It is 1420 mm.

Move the slide three numbers to the right to give meters. The length is 1.42 m.

Show a weight in two different units. Here the slide is showing a weight of 315 g.

Move the slide three numbers to the right to give kilograms. The weight is 0.315 kg.

Units

You can use these letters to stand for units instead of writing the full names of the units.

Length and weight can be measured in different units as above. These units are related as follows.

Meter = m
Centimeter = cm
Millimeter = mm
Gram = g
Kilogram = kg

1 m = 100 cm OR 1000 mm
1 cm = 10 mm OR 0.01 m
1 mm = 0.1 cm OR 0.001 m
1 kg = 1000 g
1 g = 0.001 kg

Make a prediction

Draw a graph and use it to forecast something that will happen in the future.

△ If the thermometer does not go up to 50 °C, take it out at the highest temperature. Make sure that a draft of air is not blowing across the pan.

Boiling time

Light a burner or switch on a hot plate on the stove. Take a thermometer and place it in a pan half filled with cold water. Next prepare a graph of time and temperature as shown. Measure the temperature of the water. Plot this measurement on the graph at zero time.

Place the pan on the stove and start timing with a watch that shows seconds. Read the temperature every 30 seconds

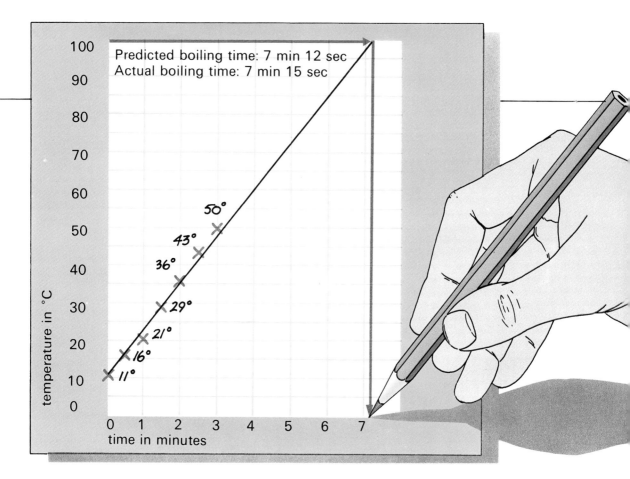

Predicted boiling time: 7 min 12 sec
Actual boiling time: 7 min 15 sec

temperature in °C

without taking the thermometer out of the water. Plot the measurements on the graph. When the thermometer reaches 50°C, take it out of the water but leave the pan on the stove. Now draw a line through the points on the graph. See where the line reaches 100°C and read the time at this point. You can predict that this is the time when the water will boil.

✹ The temperature of the water increases steadily until it boils. The graph therefore shows the temperature of the water at any time up to the point at which it boils.

△ If the points are not exactly in line, draw a straight line that goes nearest to all of them. The boiling time is the time at which the water reaches 100°C. This is when *all* the water in the pan starts to bubble. If you have made careful measurements, your prediction should be correct to within a few seconds. Graphs can be used in this way to make measurements beyond the range of measuring instruments.

13

Calculate and check

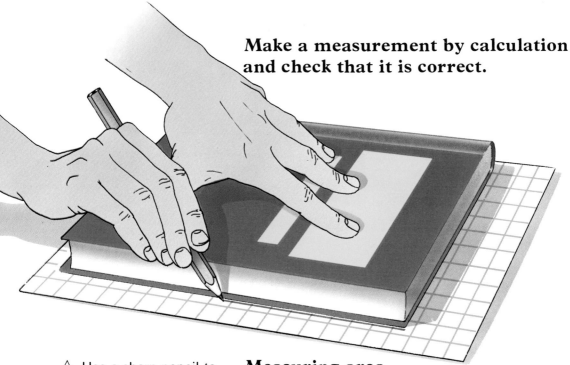

Make a measurement by calculation and check that it is correct.

△ Use a sharp pencil to draw around the book, and hold the book firmly so that it does not move.

Measuring area

Take a rectangular object like a small book. Measure its length and width and multiply them together. This gives the surface area of the book. Now check that this result is correct. Lay the book on some graph paper ruled in centimeters so that the edges line up with the lines on the paper. Then draw the outline of the book. Count the number of whole squares inside the rectangle. Then add up the incomplete squares as shown in the example. Add the two figures together and you have a direct measurement of the area.

The area of the surface of any object is the number of square centimeters or square meters in it. Using the formula *area = length × width* enables you to calculate large areas such as the area of the floor of a room. It saves you having to count up the number of square units in the floor.

▽ Doing the calculation is quick but the answer may not be very accurate. It depends on how accurately you measure the lengths. The calculated area here is best given as 187 sq cm not 187.25.

Example

The sides of the book measure 10.7 cm and 17.5 cm. The area by calculation is $10.7 \times 17.5 = 187.25$ sq cm.

On the graph paper, each square is equal to 1 sq cm. There are 170 whole squares. The incomplete squares are 10 at 0.5, one at 0.35 and 17 at 0.7. The total area of the incomplete squares comes to 17.25, so the area of the book is $170 + 17.25 = 187.25$ sq cm. So measuring the area directly gives the same answer as calculating it.

1
2
3
4
5
6
7
8
9
10 20 30 40 50 60 70 80 90 100 110 120 130 140 150 160 170

0.5

0.35

0.7

How high is that tree?

Find the height of any tree, no matter how tall.

△ Measure the size of the tree as it appears against the ruler. This is the apparent height. Take care not to move the ruler or your head as your friend measures the distance from the ruler to your eye.

The circumference of the wheel is the distance right around the outside edge of the wheel.

Simple survey

Stand some distance from the tree. Measure the apparent height of the tree with a ruler as shown. Get a friend to measure the distance from the ruler to your eye. Next measure the distance from where you are standing to the base of the tree. Do this by rolling a wheel such as a bicycle wheel to the tree and counting the number of turns. Estimate the fraction of the last turn if it is incomplete. Lastly, measure the circumference of the wheel with a tape measure and work out the height of the tree as shown in the example.

16

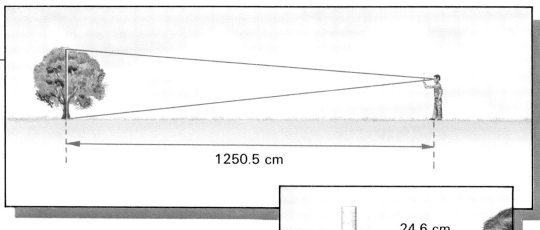

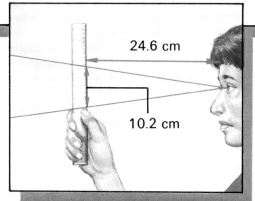

1250.5 cm

24.6 cm

10.2 cm

△ The heights and the distances make two triangles as shown in red. Both triangles are exactly the same shape.

✹ The height of the tree can be calculated because the real and apparent heights have the same proportion as the two distances measured. Surveyors use a similar method to measure heights and distances in order to make maps and plans.

△ We measure the size of the small triangle and find how much bigger the large triangle is. We can then work out the size of the large triangle and get the height of the tree.

Example

Apparent height = 10.2 cm.
Distance from ruler to eye = 24.6 cm.
Number of turns of wheel = 12.2.
Circumference of wheel = 102.5 cm.
Distance to the tree equals 12.2 × 102.5 = 1250.5 cm.

The proportion of the two distances equals 1250.5 ÷ 24.6 = 50.83. The proportion of the two heights is the same. The real height of the tree is therefore 10.2 × 50.83 = 518 cm. The method is not quite this accurate, and the result is best given as 5.2 meters.

Measuring speed

How fast can people run? Measure
distance and time to find out.

Running chart

Mark out a circular running track of about
50 to 100 meters. Ask two friends to run
around the track for a certain number of
laps. Use a watch to time both runners and
write down the times when each completes
a lap. Then work out the speed of each
runner for each lap, as shown in the
example, and draw a bar chart to compare
the speeds.

△ One person can run
while the others time
each lap. To find the
average speed, do not
add up the speeds of
each lap and divide by
the total number of laps.
Divide the *total* distance
run by the time taken.

Example

The circuit was 50 meters long, and David and Lucy took these times in seconds to run four laps:

Lap	1	2	3	4
David	10	21	35	50
Lucy	12	24	37	48

Subtract these times from each other to find the time of each lap. For example, Lucy ran lap 3 in $37 - 24 = 13$ seconds. Divide the length of the circuit by these lap times to get the speed of each lap in meters per second (m/s).

Lap	1	2	3	4
David	5.0	4.5	3.6	3.3
Lucy	4.2	4.2	3.8	4.5

Find the average speed of each runner by dividing the total distance run by the total time taken.

Average speed

David $200 \text{ m} \div 50 \text{ s} = 4.00 \text{ m/s}$
Lucy $200 \text{ m} \div 48 \text{ s} = 4.16 \text{ m/s}$

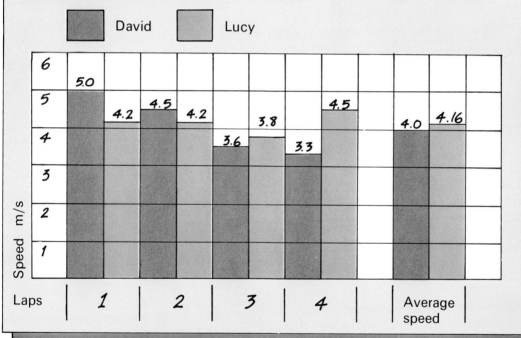

David   Lucy

Speed m/s

Laps | 1 | 2 | 3 | 4 | Average speed

✳ Speed is equal to the distance divided by the time. As there is no instrument to measure the speed of the runners, it has to be worked out from measurements of the distances run and the times taken to run them.

△ The bar chart shows that Lucy had the fastest average speed. However, David ran two of the laps faster.

Calculate a constant

Make difficult measurements easy by using a constant such as pi.

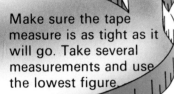

Make sure the tape measure is as tight as it will go. Take several measurements and use the lowest figure.

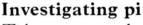

Investigating pi

Take a cup or glass with straight sides and a circular base. Measure the circumference of the base, then place the cup or glass on graph paper and draw around it. Measure the diameter of this circle. Divide the circumference by the diameter. You should get a value of about 3.14. Repeat this with other circular objects; the value is always constant (the same) for a true circle. The figure is therefore called a constant and it is given the name pi. Measure the area of the circle in the same way as the area of the book on page 15. Then calculate it using pi as shown in the example. The result should be the same.

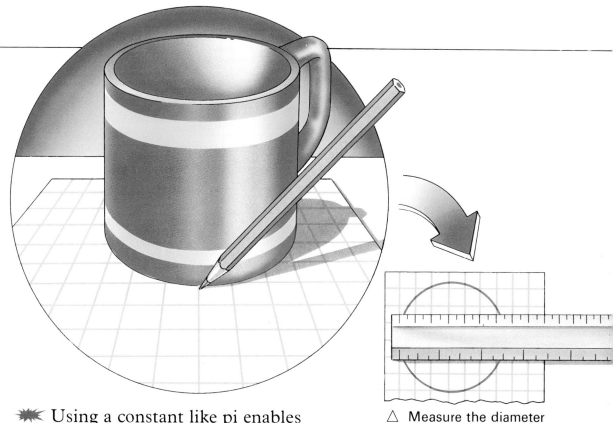

✳ Using a constant like pi enables difficult measurements to be made by simple calculations. This allows us to find out the areas and volumes of round objects.

△ Measure the diameter across the inside of the circle. Make several measurements and take the largest value that you get.

Example

Circumference = 20.7 cm.
Diameter = 6.6 cm.
Calculated value of pi equals
20.7 ÷ 6.6 = 3.14.
Formula for area of circle = *pi × radius × radius* (radius is half diameter). Calculated area equals

3.14 × 3.3 × 3.3 = 34.2 sq cm.
Measured area equals 23 whole squares plus 11.5 incomplete squares = 34.5 sq cm. This result is near enough to the calculated area to show that using pi in this way does in fact give the area.

Measure the pressure

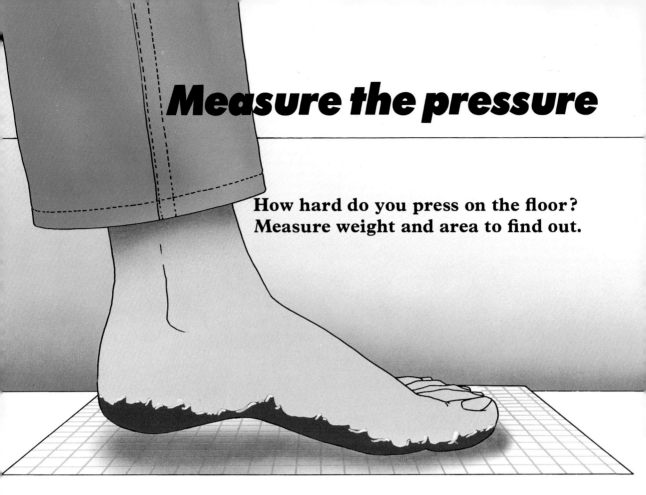

**How hard do you press on the floor?
Measure weight and area to find out.**

△ Stand on the graph paper just as you normally stand, and be sure not to move as you make the footprint.

Foot firmly on the floor

Take off your shoes and socks and get a friend to paint the bottom of one foot with poster paint. Then press this foot firmly on some graph paper. Wash the paint off your foot while the paint dries on the paper. Then measure the area of your footprint as described on page 15. Find your weight and divide it by the area as shown in the example. This is the pressure that you exert on the floor as you walk or stand on one leg. Find the foot pressures of your friends. It's possible that the heaviest person does not exert the greatest pressure if he or she has big feet.

22

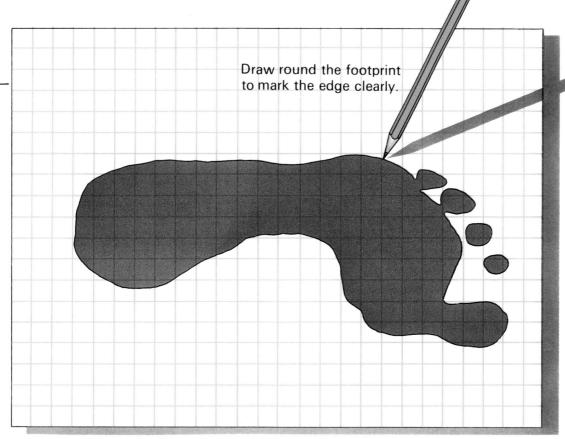

Draw round the footprint to mark the edge clearly.

✳ Pressure is equal to the weight of an object divided by the area that presses on a surface. If two people have the same weight but different foot sizes, the person with the smallest foot exerts more pressure. The method gives the average pressure for the whole foot.

△ Unless you have flat feet, your footprint shows that only a part of your foot presses on the floor. Flatfooted people therefore exert less pressure.

Example

Area of foot equals 69 whole squares plus 36.4 incomplete squares = 105.4 sq cm. Weight = 38.5 kg.

Using the formula *pressure = weight ÷ area*, the foot pressure

equals 38.5 ÷ 105.6 = 0.365 kg/sq cm. This means that on every square centimeter of floor, your foot pushes down with an average weight of 0.365 kilograms or 365 grams (about a third of air pressure).

Find the volume

How big is an object? Find out by calculation or by direct measurement.

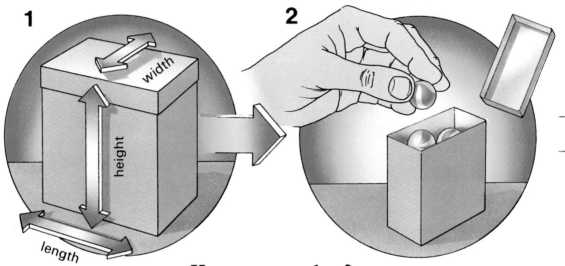

1
width
height
length

2

△ **1** Measure along the edges of the tin to get the length, width and height.
2 Fill the tin with marbles to make it sink. Push the lid fully back on.

How many cubes?
Take a tin with rectangular sides and a lid. Measure its length, width and height. Multiply these three figures together to calculate the volume of the tin. Next check the volume with a different method. Place a container in a bowl and fill the container to the brim with water. Then gently place the tin in the container so that water overflows as the tin sinks. Remove the container, being careful not to spill any more water. Then pour the water from the bowl into a measure. The volume of this water is equal to the volume of the tin.

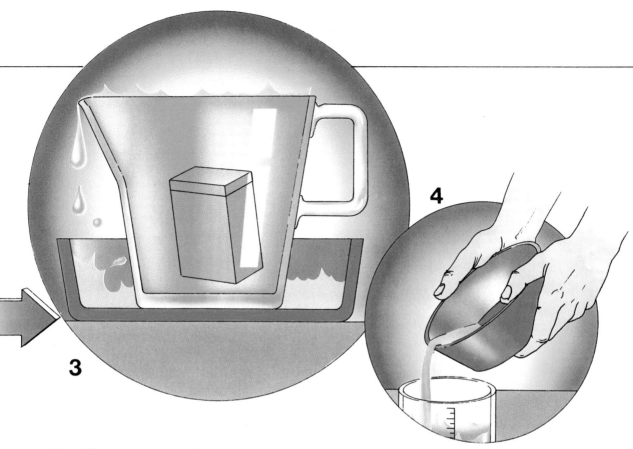

4

3

✳ The volume of the tin is equal to the number of cubes each a centimeter across that could fit into the tin. As the tin sinks, it pushes the same volume of water out of the container. This method of sinking objects in water can be used to find the volume of an object of any shape.

△ **3** Don't put your fingers in the water when you lower the tin into the container.
4 Find the volume by reading the level of the water against the scale.

Example

Length = 5 cm; width = 3.5 cm; height = 6.9 cm.
Using the formula *volume = length × width × height,* calculated volume equals 5 × 3.5 × 6.9 =

120.75 cc (cubic centimeters).
Volume of water = 120 cc.
Because neither method is very accurate, we can say the volume is 120 cc measured in both ways.

Measure and explain

△ Use scales with a pan that can hold some water. First weigh the stone or the orange.

▷ Next place a container full of water in an empty bowl. Without wetting your fingers, gently lower the stone or orange into the water so that some water overflows. Then remove the container.

Make measurements to find out why one object floats and another sinks.

How much water?

Weigh a stone on some kitchen scales and then sink the stone in water as described on page 24. Now weigh the amount of water displaced by the stone. Do this by pouring the displaced water into the pan of the scales. Be careful not to spill any of the water. You will find that the weight of the displaced water is less than the weight of the stone. Then repeat the experiment using an object that floats, such as an orange, instead of a stone. The water displaced by the orange weighs the same as the orange.

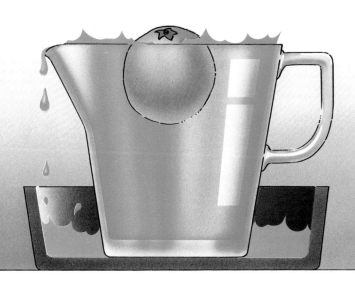

✳ This experiment shows that an object floats if the weight of water it displaces is the same as its own weight. If it weighs more than the water displaced, it sinks. Measurements are made in science to find explanations in this way. They show that correct explanations are always true.

△ Finally, pour the water from the bowl into the pan and weigh the water.

Example

Weight of stone = 370 g.
Weight of water displaced by stone = 150 g, which is less than the weight of the stone.
Weight of orange = 290 g.
Weight of water displaced by orange = 290 g, which is equal to the weight of the orange.
The object which sank therefore displaced an amount of water that weighed less than the object. The object which floated displaced an amount of water equal to its own weight.

How much does the air in a room weigh – as much as a person?

△ Measure the walls and floor by following a straight line along them with the rule or tape measure. Another way is to measure the bases and corners of the walls.

Calculate the weight

You cannot put the air in a room on scales, but you can easily calculate its weight. Using a tape measure or long rule, measure the length, width and height of a room in meters. Then multiply the three figures together to find the volume of the room in cubic meters. If the floor is not rectangular, mark it out into rectangular sections and measure the length and width of each one. Calculate the volume of each section and add the volumes together to get the volume of the room. Then multiply the volume of the room by 1.2. The result is the weight of the air in the room in kilograms.

✴ We can calculate the weight of any volume of air because we know that the weight of a cubic meter of air is 1.2 kilograms. This figure, the density of air, has been discovered by scientists. So if we measure how many cubic meters of air there are, we can find its weight.

Example

Height of room = 2.23 m; length = 5.65 m; width = 4.8 m.
Using the formula *volume = length × width × height,* volume of room equals 2.23 × 5.65 × 4.8 = 60.5 cu m (cubic meters).
Weight of air = 60.5 × 1.2 = 72.6 kg.
This figure is approximate because the weight of air depends on the pressure and temperature of the air and how dry it is. However it shows that even in a small room, the air weighs as much as or more than an adult.

△ Check your weight to see if you weigh more than the air in the room. It's unlikely that you do.

29

Facts and figures

Formulas and units

Area = length × width
Units: square millimeters (sq mm or mm²), square centimeters (sq cm or cm², square meters (sq m or m²).
1 sq cm = 100 sq mm.
1 sq m = 10,000 sq cm.

Volume = length × width × height
Units: cubic millimeters (cu mm or mm³), cubic centimeters (cc, cu cm or cm³), cubic meters (cu m or m³).
1 cu cm = 1,000 cu mm.
1 cu m = 1,000,000 cu cm.
Volume or capacity is also measured in liters (l) and milliliters (ml).
1 ml = 1 cc. 1 l = 1,000 ml or 1,000 cc.

Speed = distance ÷ time
Units: meters per second (m/s), kilometers per hour (km/hr).
1 m/s = 3.6 km/hr.
1 km/hr = 0.278 m/s.

Pressure = weight ÷ area
Units: kilograms per square centimeter (kg/sq cm).

Pressure of air is approximately 1 kg/sq cm.

Density = weight ÷ volume
Units: grams per cubic centimeter (g/cc), kilograms per cubic meter (kg/cu m).
Density of water = 1 g/cc. Density of air is approximately 1.2 kg/cu m.

Basic units

Weight
Units: grams (g), kilograms (kg), tonnes.
1 tonne = 1,000 kg.
1 kg = 1,000 g.
Weight of Earth is approximately 6 million million million tonnes.

Length
Units: millimeter (mm), centimeter (cm), meter (m), kilometer (km).
1 km = 1,000 m. 1 m = 100 cm. 1 cm = 10 mm.
Circumference of Earth is approximately 40,000 km.

Time
Units: seconds (s), minutes (min), hours (hr), days.
1 day = 24 hr. 1 hr = 60 min. 1 min = 60 s.
Length of year = 365 days, 6 hr, 9 min, 9.5 s.

Calculation and accuracy

When any calculation is made with measurements, it is important to think about how accurate the result will be. Say that the calculation is multiplying 12.8 times 32.7. A calculator gives the answer 418.56. Now, if the measurements are made to one figure after the decimal point, then the result cannot be any more accurate than this. The very best that you can say is that the result is 418.6. In fact, 419 (the nearest whole number) is probably the most accurate result possible. Calculators often give answers to many decimal places. Remember that they can never be this accurate: use only the first three or four numbers shown.

Conversion tables

Metric to Standard	Standard to Metric

Weight
1 gram (g) =0.035 ounces
1 kilogram (kg) =2.2 pounds
1 tonne =2,204 pounds

Length
1 centimeter (cm) =0.39 inches
1 meter (m) =39.37 inches
1 kilometer (km) =0.62 miles

Area
1 square centimeter (sq cm) = 0.155 square inches
1 square meter (sq m) =1,550 square inches
1 square kilometer (sq km) = 0.386 square miles

Volume
1 cubic centimeter (cu cm) = 0.061 cubic inches
1 cubic meter (cu m) =35.31 cubic feet

Capacity
1 liter (l) =2.11 pints or 0.264 gallons

Temperature
1 °C =9/5 °F.
To convert °C to °F, multiply by 9/5 and add 32.

Weight
1 ounce (oz) =28.3 grams
1 pound (lb) =453.6 grams
1 ton =907.2 kilograms

Length
1 inch (in) =2.54 centimeters
1 foot (ft) =30.48 centimeters
1 mile (mi) =1.61 kilometers

Area
1 square inch (sq in) =6.45 square centimeters
1 square foot (sq ft) =0.093 square meters
1 square mile (sq mi) =2.59 square kilometers

Volume
1 cubic inch (cu in) =16.39 cubic centimeters
1 cubic foot (cu ft) =0.028 cubic meters

Capacity
1 pint (pt) =473 milliliters
1 gallon (gal) =3.79 liters

Temperature
1 °F =5/9 °C
To convert °F to °C, subtract 32 and multiply by 5/9.

Index